Marine Mammals

SEA OTTERS

ZELDA KING

PowerKiDS press.
New York

Published in 2012 by The Rosen Publishing Group, Inc.
29 East 21st Street, New York, NY 10010

First Edition

Editor: Joanne Randolph
Book Design: Julio Gil

Photo Credits: Cover David Courtenay/Getty Images; pp. 4, 5, 6, 10–11, 12, 15, 16, 17, 18 (top) Shutterstock.com; p. 7 Wikimedia Commons; p. 8 Bates Littlehales/National Geographic/Getty Images; p. 9 © www.iStockphoto.com/Nicole S. Young; p. 13 Yoshikazu Tsuno/AFP/Getty Images; pp. 14 (top, bottom), 22 iStockphoto/Thinkstock; p. 18 (bottom) © www.iStockphoto.com/Tom O'Connell; p. 19 Daniel Cox/Oxford Scientific/Getty Images; p. 20 © www.iStockphoto.com/Richard Seeley; p. 21 © Alaska Stock/age fotostock.

Library of Congress Cataloging-in-Publication Data

King, Zelda.
Sea otters / by Zelda King. — 1st ed.
p. cm. — (Marine mammals)
Includes index.
ISBN 978-1-4488-5004-4 (library binding) — ISBN 978-1-4488-5139-3 (pbk.) —
ISBN 978-1-4488-5140-9 (6-pack)
1. Sea otter—Juvenile literature. I. Title. II. Series.
QL737.C25K5823 2012
599.769'5—dc22

2010048085

Manufactured in the United States of America

CPSIA Compliance Information: Batch #WS11PK: For Further Information contact Rosen Publishing, New York, New York at 1-800-237-9932

CONTENTS

Say Hello to Sea Otters 4
Prowling the Pacific Ocean 6
Home, Sweet Home 8
The Smallest Marine Mammal 10
What Makes It a Mammal? 12
Fabulous Fur 14
What Sea Otters Eat 16
Days of Drifting, Eating, and Grooming ... 18
The Life of a Sea Otter 20
Saving Sea Otters 22
Glossary 23
Index 24
Web Sites 24

Say Hello to Sea Otters

Have you ever seen a sea otter? Many people enjoy viewing these **marine** animals at aquariums. The cute, furry **mammals** spend much of their time floating on top of the water. That makes it easy for people to watch them.

Did You Know?

Sea otters belong to a big animal family. It includes otters that live in rivers and lakes. It also includes land animals such as weasels, badgers, and skunks!

Most animals swim on their stomachs. Sea otters can, too. They spend much of their time swimming and floating on their backs, though. They use their back paws and strong tails to swim this way.

How do otters eat if they are lying on their backs most of the time? They use their chests as tables! Mother sea otters even carry their babies on their chests.

Left: Sea otters, such as these two, can live up to 23 years in the wild. There are likely between 80,000 and 120,000 sea otters swimming in the Pacific Ocean.

Right: This is a weasel. Weasels are related to otters. They live on land, though, not in the ocean.

Prowling the Pacific Ocean

Some marine mammals live in oceans around the world. However, sea otters are found in only one. All the wild sea otters in the world live in the northern Pacific Ocean. Some live near Asia. A very few, maybe only 10 or 12, live near Japan. About 15,000 of them live along the northern coast of Russia.

The rest of the world's sea otters live near North America. About

This otter lives in the icy waters near Alaska. Those waters are cold! The sea otter counts on its fur to keep its body warm and dry.

Where Sea Otters Live

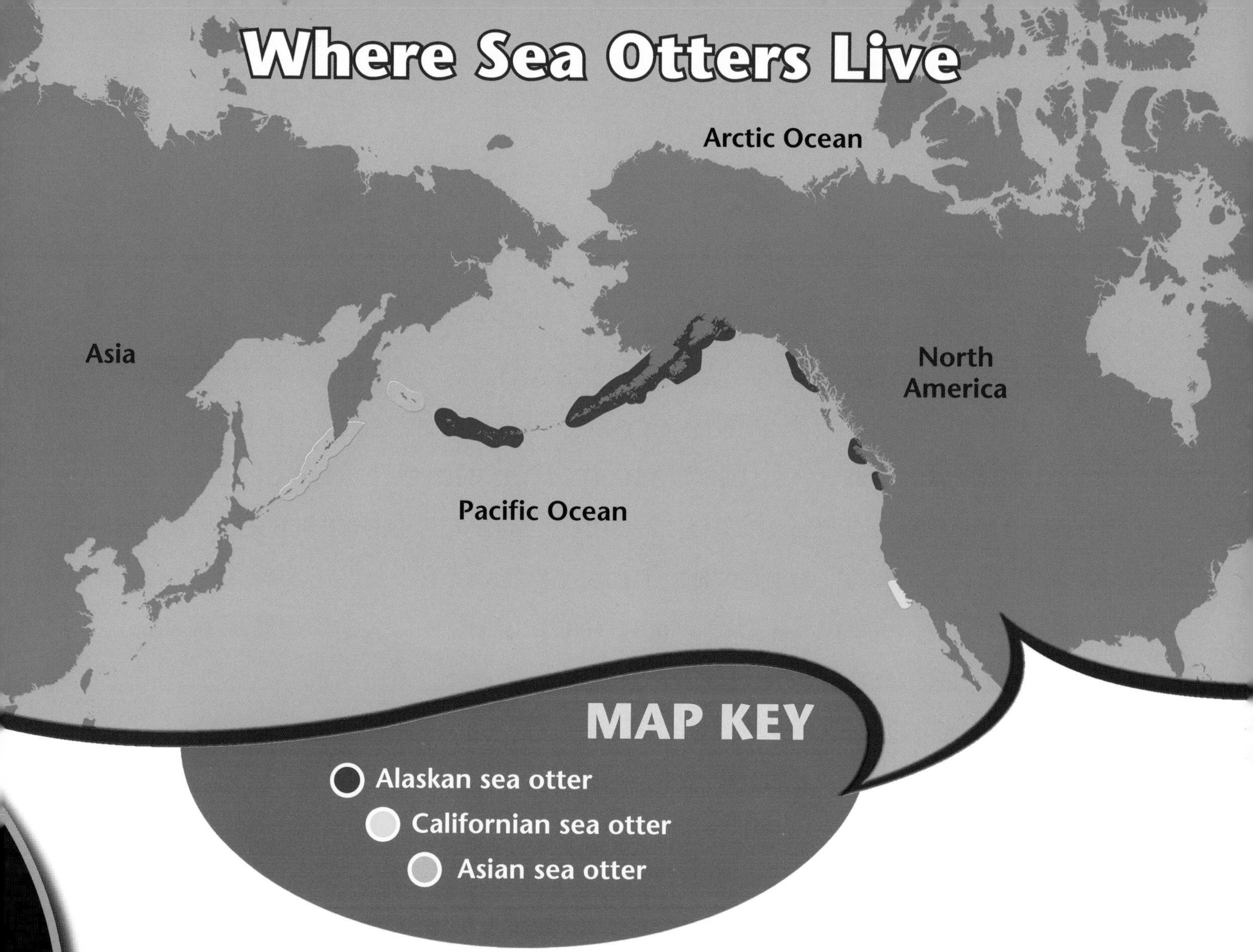

Arctic Ocean
Asia
North America
Pacific Ocean

MAP KEY
Alaskan sea otter
Californian sea otter
Asian sea otter

3,000 are found along the coast of California. The largest sea otter population in the world lives around Alaska, Washington State, and northwestern Canada. There are about 70,000 sea otters there!

Home, Sweet Home

Since sea otters are marine mammals, you might expect them to live far out in the ocean. However, sea otters like to live in **shallow** water close to the shore. Most of the time, they are only about .5 mile (805 m) from shore.

Why do sea otters favor shallow coastal waters? It is because the food they like lives on the ocean bottom. Sea otters must dive down to get their food. They cannot

This sea otter is diving down to the ocean bottom to find food. Sea otters eat about 160 different kinds of food, including starfish.

hold their breath for very long, so they want to live where they do not have to make deep dives.

The sea otter's food commonly lives on rocky or sandy ocean bottoms and among kelp forests. Sea otters always live in habitats with these features.

Sea otters are often found in kelp beds, such as this one. Kelp beds are home to many foods they like to eat.

The Smallest Marine Mammal

The sea otter is the smallest marine mammal in North America. Males are commonly 4 to 5 feet (1–1.5 m) long and weigh 60 to 85 pounds (27–39 kg). Females are smaller. Sea otters have thick, dark fur. The fur on their heads, throats, and chests is a lighter color. They have short front legs. Their long back legs have wide, flat paws. These paws are **webbed** for swimming.

The sea otter's round head has a big nose and small, widely spaced eyes. Like people's, the sea otter's ears are on the sides of its head.

Did You Know?

Long ago, hunters killed so many sea otters they were almost gone. Luckily, their numbers are growing again in some places.

Sea otters are the heaviest members of the weasel family, but they are small for marine mammals. Other marine mammals include walruses, dolphins, and whales.

What Makes It a Mammal?

When you imagine ocean animals, do you first picture animals such as fish, clams, and octopuses? These animals and others like them are **cold-blooded**. Many lack a backbone. They eat and breathe underwater. Take them out of water, and they die. Sea otters are different. They are mammals, just as you are.

How do we know sea otters are mammals? They have all the marks of mammals. Sea otters have thick fur. They

Many animals that live in the ocean are not mammals, such as this octopus. It has no fur, breathes underwater, and has no backbone.

cannot stay underwater for long but must come up to breathe air. Sea otters are **warm-blooded** and have a backbone. Females also feed milk to their young, just as all mammal species do.

Here a sea otter mother floats with her pup on her stomach. Their thick fur keeps them warm in the cold water where they live.

Fabulous Fur

Sea otters have wonderful fur. They have a thick, soft undercoat and an outer coat of long hairs called guard hairs. Their fur is usually gray, brown, or reddish brown.

The sea otter's fur is very thick. About one million hairs grow out of 1 square inch (6 sq cm) of skin. That is

Sea otters' fur keeps their skin warm and dry. This is important since water takes heat away from a body 25 times faster than air does!

Sea otters groom their fur to keep it in great shape. Sea otters do not shed their fur all at once. They shed a little bit all year long.

about 10 times as much hair as you have on your whole head!

Why do sea otters have such thick fur? They need it to keep warm in cold water. Most marine mammals have thick fat under their skin for warmth. Sea otters do not.

What Sea Otters Eat

Sea otters eat only ocean animals. They dine on starfish, octopuses, crabs, snails, fish, and **sea urchins**. They also eat **mollusks** such as clams, mussels, and abalones. Would you enjoy a sea otter's meal?

Sea otters have a neat trick for carrying food up from the ocean bottom. They tuck it into loose skin folds under their armpits! Then they eat while floating on their backs.

Sea otters are the only marine mammals that catch fish with their hands rather than their teeth. Their teeth are better for crushing than for grabbing or cutting.

You might wonder how sea otters open mollusk shells. They use tools! They put rocks on their chests and pound the mollusks on them until the shells break open.

This sea otter has caught a crab. Sea otters need to eat a lot of food to help keep their bodies warm.

Days of Drifting, Eating, and Grooming

How much time do you spend eating every day? Sea otters spend up to 12 hours each day looking for food and filling their bellies! That is because they need to eat about one-quarter of their body weight in food each day to stay warm. You likely do not spend very long cleaning yourself every day, either.

Above: Sea otters use their front paws to hold food and put it in their mouths. The paws have pads that let the otters hold on to their meals. *Right*: When resting, sea otters hold their front and back paws against their bodies to keep in more warmth.

This mother and baby otter are taking a break on a kelp bed. Kelp beds can be above water at low tides.

Sea otters spend about three hours each day **grooming** themselves! Their fur must be clean in order to keep them warm. They roll in the water, rub their fur with their paws, and blow air into it.

Sea otters also find time to play and sleep. When they sleep, they wrap themselves in **kelp** growing from the seafloor so they do not drift away!

The Life of a Sea Otter

Sea otters generally live about 10 to 20 years. They are born at sea, and many never come ashore.

Commonly, a mother has one pup at a time. She feeds it, grooms it, and carries it on her chest. When she dives for food, she wraps the pup in kelp so it does not float away.

Mothers and pups live in groups, called rafts. Pups stay with their mothers for about six months. They learn how to swim,

Mother sea otters teach their pups all the skills they will need to live on their own.

groom themselves, and find food. They are grown and ready to have their own pups when they are about five years old.

Did You Know?

The sea otter's thick undercoat traps air bubbles in it. The air holds in the heat produced by the sea otter's body and keeps out the water and the cold.

Here a raft of sea otters floats off the coast of Alaska. Male sea otters form separate rafts from those of females and young.

Saving Sea Otters

Sea otters once almost became **extinct** because people hunted them for their fur and meat. Today it is unlawful for most people to hunt them. They face other dangers, though. Natural enemies include killer whales and sharks. The whales attack sea otters because seals, their usual food, are disappearing.

People also harm sea otters. They build along coasts and destroy sea otter **habitats**. Fishing nets catch sea otters and drown them. Ocean **pollution** harms sea otters and kills the animals that are their food. Oil spilled in the ocean makes sea otters sick and harms their coats. They may die from the cold. We must guard sea otters and their habitats so they do not disappear forever.

Sea otters are interesting animals. Do you want to learn more about them?

GLOSSARY

cold-blooded (KOHLD-bluh-did) Having a body heat that changes with the surrounding heat.

extinct (ik-STINGKT) No longer existing.

grooming (GROOM-ing) Cleaning the body and making it appear neat.

habitats (HA-beh-tats) The surroundings where an animal or a plant naturally lives.

kelp (KELP) A large, brown seaweed.

mammals (MA-mulz) Warm-blooded animals that have a backbone and hair, breathe air, and feed milk to their young.

marine (muh-REEN) Having to do with the sea.

mollusks (MAH-lusks) Animals without backbones and with soft bodies and, often, shells.

pollution (puh-LOO-shun) Manmade waste that harms Earth's air, land, or water.

sea urchins (SEE UR-chinz) Small sea animals with hard shells and hard, pointy spines.

shallow (SHA-loh) Not deep.

warm-blooded (WORM-bluh-did) Having a body heat that stays the same, no matter how warm or cold the surroundings are.

webbed (WEBD) Having skin between the toes, as do ducks, frogs, and other animals that swim.

INDEX

A
Asia, 6

B
babies, 5
backbone, 12–13
back(s), 5, 16

C
California, 7
Canada, 7
chest(s), 5, 10, 17, 20
coast(s), 6–7, 22

H
habitats, 22

J
Japan, 6

K
kelp, 19–20

M
mollusks, 16–17

N
North America, 6, 10

P
paws, 5, 10, 19
people, 4, 22
pollution, 22
population, 7

R
Russia, 6

S
sea urchins, 16
stomachs, 5

T
tables, 5
tails, 5

W
Washington State, 7
water(s), 4, 8, 12, 15, 19

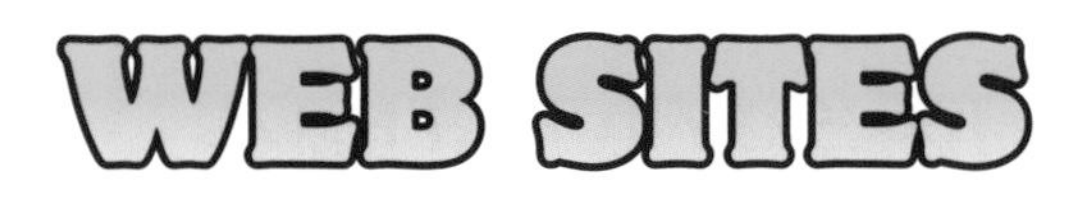

Due to the changing nature of Internet links, PowerKids Press has developed an online list of Web sites related to the subject of this book. This site is updated regularly. Please use this link to access the list:
www.powerkidslinks.com/marm/seaotter/